SECOND EDITION

Super Practice Book

3

**Garan Holcombe**

T0349652

CAMBRIDGE
UNIVERSITY PRESS

# Map of the book

# Be good at + ing

Oliver   Daisy   George

Sophie   Lucy

What about you, Lucy?
What are you good at doing?

I'm good at singing. Would you like me to sing a song, Mr Simmons?

**Language focus**

Use **be good at + ing** to talk about something that we can or can't do well.

*Maggie is good at playing football, but she isn't good at going to bed at the right time.*

**1** **Make six sentences about you and your friends using the information.**

| I'm | good at | climbing trees. |
| | | painting. |
| He's | | cooking. |
| | | swimming. |
| She's | not good at | playing tennis. |
| | | dancing. |
| They're | | running. |

1  I'm good at cooking.

2  _____

3  _____

4  _____

5  _____

6  _____

**2** Match sentences 1–6 with sentences a–f.

MEET THE TEACHERS NIGHT

1 One day he will play for Barcelona!

2 The horses listen to her!

3 Her paintings are like Picasso's!

4 She's so fast! 100 metres in 15 seconds!

5 He can play Beethoven, Bach and Mozart!

6 He makes great chicken and rice!

a Yes, Mr Martins. Jon is very good at cooking.

b Yes, Mrs Thomas. David is very good at playing the piano.

c Yes, Mr Scott. Carla is very good at running.

d Yes, Mrs Hatton. Richard is very good at playing football.

e Yes, Mr Doyle. Alice is very good at painting.

f Yes, Mrs Simpson. Rachel's good at horse riding.

**3** Look at the pictures. Then complete the sentences using *is good at* / *is not good at* and a verb from the box in the *ing* form.

ask   skate   write   ~~play~~   snorkel

1 Anna **is not good at playing** the violin.

2 Bill _____ in the sea.

3 Milly _____ fast.

4 Suzie _____ stories.

5 Jake _____ questions.

# Possessive apostrophe

I love that house, Bobby!

Me too! It's my brother's house. It's near the sea!

**Language focus**

Use the **possessive apostrophe** to say that one person is related to another or that something belongs to someone.

*Sean's kite is blue and red.* (Sean's kite = the kite of Sean)

*Jane's bike is new.* (Jane's bike = the bike of Jane)

*Connor's father works in New York.* (Connor's father = the father of Connor)

**1** Tick ✓ the correct sentences. Underline the mistakes. Then write the correct sentences.

1 Bens mother is called Kim. ☒ Ben's mother is called Kim.

2 Marta's father is good at drawing. ☐ _____

3 Sams sister is five years old. ☐ _____

4 Ron's uncle is a tennis player. ☐ _____

5 Tonys brother runs really fast. ☐ _____

6 Janes grandmother speaks Chinese and Spanish. ☐ _____

_____

**2** Add four possessive apostrophes to the blog post so that it reads correctly.

## OUR FAVOURITE THINGS

Everyone has got favourite things. My sister's favourite thing is her computer. It's new. There is only one thing my brother loves – his guitar! He plays it all the time. My brothers guitar is a Fender Stratocaster. My father doesn't like guitars. He likes bikes! My fathers bike is very old. Dad doesn't know it, but I don't like his bike. I don't think Mum likes it either. Her favourite thing is her car. Mums car is blue. Do you know what I like best? My dog! He's called Bernard. Bernards favourite things are my shoes. He loves eating them!

**3** Look at Ben's family tree and answer the questions.

1 Who is Penny?
  Penny is Ben <u>'s sister</u> .

2 Who is Ted?
  Ted is Penny and Ben _____ .

3 Who is Maria?
  Maria is Paula _____ .

4 Who is Oliver?
  Oliver is Penny _____ .

5 Who is Paula?
  Paula is Molly _____ .

Ben's Family

Bob | Julia

Ted    Maria        Oliver   Lisa

Penny    Ben        Paula    Molly

**4** Write five sentences of your own about Ben's family. Remember to use possessive apostrophes!

1 _____

2 _____

3 _____

4 _____

5 _____

# Reading: a diary

**1** Read Clara's diary and complete the text with the names from the box.

## FEBRUARY

**2** TUESDAY
Week 5

Oh dear. I'm not good at doing anything. Everyone is good at doing something, but not me. My friends, for example, are good at doing lots of different things. Jenny's good at dancing. She's good at cooking too. She makes great tomato sauce!

Mark is good at running, singing, playing the piano and doing his homework. Mark's brother, Tony, is good at writing stories and playing football. Olga is good at doing Science and drawing. Lola is good at painting and doing puzzles. Oh, Lola is good at everything! She's good at climbing and jumping and swimming. I want to be Lola!

I'm not good at doing anything. No, that's wrong! I am good at doing one thing: writing my diary!

Jenny   Clara   Lola   Mark   ~~Tony~~   Olga

Clara's friends are good at doing lots of things. (1) __Tony__ is good at playing football. (2) _____ is good at doing puzzles. (3) _____ is good at doing his homework. (4) _____ is good at making tomato sauce. (5) _____ is good at drawing. (6) _____ says she is good at doing only one thing.

**1** **Complete the sentences with the correct family words.**

1 Your mother's brother is your _____uncle_____ .

2 Your father's son is your _____ .

3 Your mother's mother is your _____ .

4 Your father's father is your _____ .

5 Your father's sister is your _____ .

6 Your uncle's daughter is your _____ .

## Help with Writing

When people write diaries, they often write about what they do, but you can also write what you feel about your life: *I'm sad because I can't find my favourite kite.*

**2** **Write a diary entry about the things you and your family are good at and not good at doing. Write about some of the family members from Activity 1.**

# FEBRUARY

### 3 WEDNESDAY
#### Week 5

_____

_____

_____

_____

_____

_____

_____

_____

_____

_____

# Listening: activities and families

**1** 🎧 01 **Listen and tick ✓ or cross ✗.**

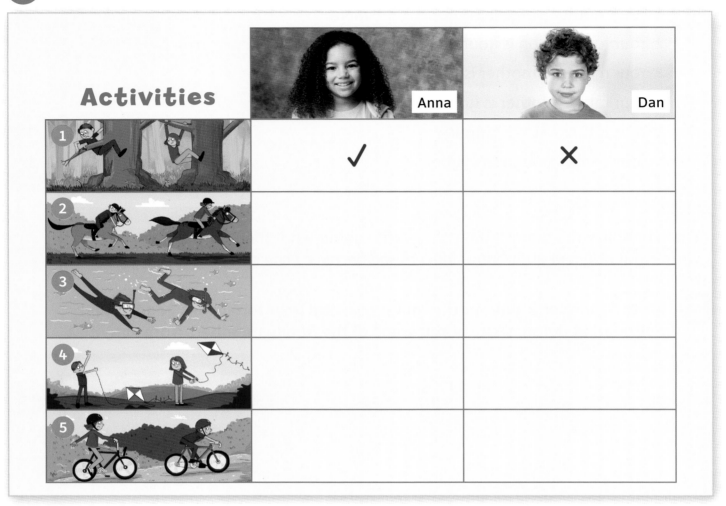

| Activities | Anna | Dan |
|---|---|---|
| 1 | ✓ | ✗ |
| 2 | | |
| 3 | | |
| 4 | | |
| 5 | | |

**2** 🎧 02 **Listen and match.**

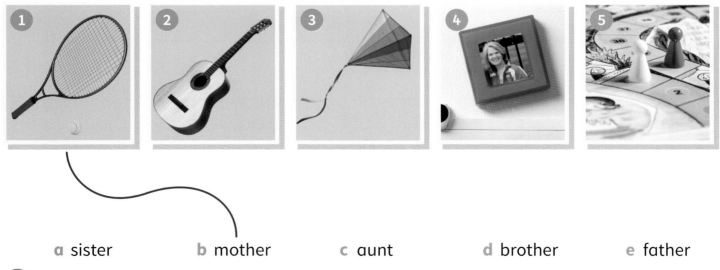

**a** sister     **b** mother     **c** aunt     **d** brother     **e** father

**1** Draw a member of your family or stick a photo into the box.

**2** Look at your picture or photo and write answers. Then practise.

1 Who's that?

That's _____. He's / She's my _____.

2 What is he / she good at?

He's / She's _____.

3 What is he / she not good at?

He / She isn't _____.

**3** Work with a friend. Ask and answer.

Who's that?

What is your aunt good at?

That's my aunt, Kim. She's my mother's sister.

She's good at running.

# 1 Like / Don't like + ing

> I like Art. It's my favourite subject. I **like drawing** and **painting**. But I really **don't like doing** Maths homework. I'm not good at it.

**Language focus**

Use **like** / **don't like + ing** to talk about what you like doing or don't like doing.

I **like reading**.

Does he / she **like eating** chocolate?   Yes, he / she does.

**1** Write sentences using *like + ing*.

## School and my family

Harry is my brother. **(1)** He like / study / Geography. My sister's name is Mila. **(2)** She / like / listen to / stories about / the past. **(3)** She / like / read / about / kings and queens too. History is her favourite subject. My name is Sam. I love English. **(4)** I like / learn / new words. What about you? **(5)** What / you / like / learn about / in school?

1   He likes studying Geography.

2   _____

3   _____

4   _____

5   _____

**2** Complete the sentences using *like + ing*.

read ~~swim~~ play (x2)

Here are some pictures of my friends doing their favourite activities. (1) Evie ___likes swimming___ . She's very good at it! (2) Eliot and Noah _____ computer games. They play their computer games for hours and hours! (3) George _____ tennis. He loves sport! (4) Ava _____ books. She is always reading! What do you like doing at the weekend?

**3** Put sentences 1–4 in Activity 1 into the negative form.

1 Evie **doesn't like swimming.** _____

2 Eliot and Noah _____

3 George _____

4 Ava _____

**4** Write four sentences about yourself and your friends using *like + ing*.

1 _____

2 _____

3 _____

4 _____

# Have to / has to + infinitive

Nia, why are you wearing those trainers? You **have to wear** your shoes to school!

## Language focus

Use **have** / **has to + infinitive** to talk about something that somebody else tells us to do.

He **has to wear** a uniform to school.

Miss Smith says we **have to study** for the History test.

Do I / you / we / they **have to do it?**    Yes, I / you / we / they do.    No, I / you / we / they don't.

Does he / she **have to do it?**    Yes, he / she does.    No, he / she doesn't.

**1**  **Complete the text with the words from the box.**

> brush (x2)   ~~do~~   finish   go   wash

Rules, rules, rules! Do your parents say, 'You have to (1) ____**do**____ your homework'? My parents say it all the time! 'Come on, Oscar,' says Dad, 'you have to (2) _____ your homework before you can watch TV.' 'Come on, Oscar,' says Mum, 'you have to (3) _____ your hands before dinner.' 'Come on, Oscar,' says Dad, 'you have to (4) _____ your teeth after dinner.' 'Come on, Oscar,' says Mum, 'you have to (5) _____ to bed at nine o'clock.' There are so many rules! Sometimes, my parents forget their own rules. For example, Dad often sits down on the sofa after dinner and watches TV. Then I say, 'Come on, Dad, you have to (6) _____ your teeth after dinner!'

**2** Match the sentence halves to complete the rules.

**English class rules**

1 You have to speak       a ten new English words every week.

2 You have to read       b your homework.

3 You have to learn       c English at all times.

4 You have to do       d your mobile phone off in class.

5 You have to listen to       e one book in English every month.

6 You have to turn       f one song a week in English.

**3** Write four rules for your English class that all the students will like. Use *have to*.

1 _____

2 _____

3 _____

4 _____

**4** Look at the pictures. Then complete the sentences using *has to* and words from the box.

~~walk~~   wear a uniform   tidy up   get up   do her homework   make breakfast

1 Alice __**has to walk**__ to school.

2 Holly _____ at six o'clock.

3 Lucas _____ for his sisters.

4 Caspar _____ his bedroom.

5 Alex _____ to school.

6 Lily _____ after school.

# Reading: an email

**1**  Read the email. Write *t* (true) or *f* (false).
Correct the false sentences.

● ● ●

To:  simona@lifemail.com

Subject:  *What I like and don't like doing*

*Hi, Simona*

*Thank you for your email and the brilliant photo!*

*You want to know what I like doing and what I don't like doing in school. Well, I love learning about the countries of the world. I also like reading about life in huge cities like Tokyo and Mexico City. I love reading stories, too. We read a story every Friday afternoon with Mr Dubois. He's my favourite teacher. He's very funny. After reading a story with Mr Dubois, we usually write a story of our own. I like writing stories, but it's not easy!*

*I don't like doing homework every night. I think we have too much homework, but the teachers say, 'You have to do your homework, Catherine!'*

*What about you, Simona? What are your favourite subjects? What do you like doing? What do you really not like doing?*

*Email soon!*

*Cathy*

1  Cathy doesn't like reading about cities.  ☑ f

   **Cathy likes reading about cities.**

2  Cathy's class reads a story every week.  ☐

   _____

3  Cathy doesn't like Mr Dubois.  ☐

   _____

4  Cathy doesn't like writing stories.  ☐

   _____

5  Cathy likes doing homework every night.  ☐

   _____

**1** Complete the table with information about you.

| | |
|---|---|
| My favourite subjects at school | |
| Things I like doing at school | |
| Things I don't like doing at school | |

## Help with Writing

When you write an email to someone you know, begin with 'Hi, _____'
or 'Hello, _____'. If you don't know the person or don't know them well,
begin with 'Dear _____'.

**2** Imagine you are Simona. Use the information in the table in Activity 1 to help you write an email to Cathy, answering all of her questions.

● ● ●

To: cathy@anglomail.com

Subject: What I like and don't like doing

Hi, Cathy

Thanks for your email! _____

_____

_____

_____

_____

_____

Email soon!

Simona

# Listening: school subjects and rules

**1** 🎧 **03** **Listen to Charlie talk about school. Circle the correct answers.**

1 Does Charlie like his teacher?

   (**a**) Yes, he does.    **b** No, he doesn't.

2 Is he good at Maths?

   **a** Yes, he is.    **b** No, he isn't.

3 Does he like Maths?

   **a** Yes, he does.    **b** No, he doesn't.

4 What is Charlie's favourite subject?

   **a** History.    **b** English.

5 Is he good at Geography?

   **a** Yes, he is.    **b** No, he isn't.

**2** 🎧 **04** **What does Lily have to do at school? Listen and tick ☑ or cross ☒.**

# Remember to ...

wear your uniform. ☑

arrive at school at eight o'clock. ☐

do your homework every day. ☐

go to a club after school. ☐

read a book every week. ☐

bring your lunch. ☐

**1** Look and write the school subject. Then play the description game.

> You draw and paint pictures.

> It's Art.

Music

_____

_____

_____

_____

_____

## Help with Speaking

In a conversation, try to listen to your friend. Ask your friend questions and use words that show interest, for example, _Really? Wow! That's great!_

**2** Work with a friend. Talk about the subjects in Activity 1.

> Do you like Music?

> Yes, I do! I like playing instruments and singing.

> Really? Me too!

**3** Write four dream rules for your English class. Then talk about your rules.

### Dream rules for English class

We have to _____ .

We don't have to _____ .

We have to _____ .

We don't have to _____ .

> We have to sing and dance every day! We don't have to do homework.

# 2 Questions and answers with *some* and *any*

**Is there any tomato juice, Ryan?**

**I can't see it. There is some orange juice and some apple juice, but I don't think there is any tomato juice.**

## Language focus

Use **some** and **any** to talk about the amount of something that there is. Use **some** in positive sentences and **any** in negatives and questions.

*There is **some** rice in the cupboard, but there aren't **any** noodles.*

*Are there **any** sandwiches?*　　*Yes, there are **some** sandwiches.*

*No, there aren't **any** sandwiches.*

### 1 Match descriptions 1–6 with pictures a–f.

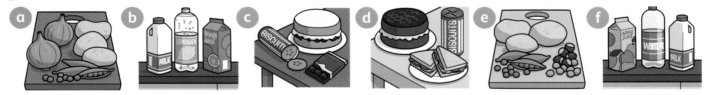

1　There is some water. There is some apple juice. There is some milk. ☑ f

2　There are some peas. There are some potatoes. There are some nuts. ☐

3　There are some biscuits. There is some cake. There is some chocolate. ☐

4　There are some potatoes. There are some peas. There are some onions. ☐

5　There is some milk. There is some lemonade. There is some orange juice. ☐

6　There is some cake. There are some biscuits. There are some sandwiches. ☐

**2** Write the questions and negative forms.

1 There is some cheese.

Is there any cheese?

There isn't any cheese.

2 There are some rolls.

3 There is some salad.

4 There are some vegetables.

5 There is some soup.

**3** Look at the picture and write sentences. Use *some* and *any*.

1 carrots **There aren't any carrots.**

2 milk

3 cheese

4 tomatoes

5 onions

6 biscuits

7 orange juice

8 peas

# Suggestions

**Shall we** make a cake for Mum's birthday, Julia?

OK! **How about** a chocolate one?

## Language focus

Use the phrases **Shall we ... ?** and **How about ... ?** to make suggestions.

*Shall we make some lunch? How about a sandwich?*

Use **Shall we** + **infinitive** not ~~Shall we + ing.~~

*Shall we go to a café?* ✔        *Shall we going to a café?* ✘

**1** Circle the correct questions. Then match questions 1–5 with pictures a–e.

1 How some cake? / (How about some cake?)

2 Shall we having some cheese? / Shall we have some cheese?

3 How about some orange juice? / Where about orange juice?

4 Shall have some sandwiches? / Shall we have some sandwiches?

5 How about any tea? / How about some tea?

e

d

a

b

c

**2** Complete the sentences with the words from the box.

> OK   about   have   ~~Shall~~   Good

Jack **(1)** ___Shall___ we make a sandwich for lunch?

Sara **(2)** _____ idea.

Jack How **(3)** _____ a chicken sandwich?

Sara **(4)** _____ .

Jack Shall we **(5)** _____ some salad with it?

Sara Yes, please! I like chicken with salad.

**3** Order the sentences in the dialogues.

**1**

☐ OK.

☐ Good idea! How about an onion and carrot one?

[1] Shall we make a pizza?

☐ Yuk! How about cheese and tomato?

**2**

☐ How about egg sandwiches, then?

☐ Shall we have sandwiches for lunch?

☐ Great idea. Oh no! There aren't any sausages in the fridge.

☐ OK. How about sausage sandwiches?

**3**

☐ Yes, of course. How about lemonade?

☐ Yes, please. I like juice.

☐ Sorry. I don't like that.

☐ I'm thirsty. Can I have a drink, please?

☐ That's OK. How about apple juice?

**4**

☐ Yes, OK. I like sausages and eggs.

☐ Yes! Good idea.

☐ Shall we have beans with it?

☐ How about sausages and eggs for breakfast?

☐ I think there are some tins in the cupboard … yes! Here they are.

**5**

☐ Yes, good idea! Oh no! There isn't any tomato soup in the cupboard.

☐ Oh dear. How about vegetable soup?

☐ That sounds great!

☐ Shall we have soup for dinner?

☐ OK! How about tomato soup?

# Reading: a blog post

**1** Read the blog post. Then complete the sentences.

## LUKA'S BRILLIANT FOOD BLOG

### Shall we visit the Soup Shop?

Hi, everyone! Today I want to talk about a great restaurant in my town. It's called the Soup Shop. The only thing you can eat there is soup! All kinds of soup. You can order sausage soup and cheese soup, mango soup and tea soup. You can also order chocolate and biscuit soup, and almost every other kind of soup. But you can't order anything else at the Soup Shop. Customers can't say, 'Excuse me, is there any pizza?' or 'Are there any chicken sandwiches?' 'No,' the waiters and waitresses say, 'there isn't any pizza. There aren't any chicken sandwiches at the Soup Shop. But there is some soup at the Soup Shop. Lots of soup! Would you like to see the menu?'

My parents and I love the Soup Shop. We go there for a meal every Friday evening. How about egg and banana soup? Do you think that's a good idea? You're right! It's yummy! It's my favourite thing to eat at the Soup Shop. You should try it! See you in the next post!

1 Excuse me, is there _____ any pizza _____?

2 There isn't _____.

3 There aren't _____ at the Soup Shop.

4 There is _____ at the Soup Shop.

5 How about _____?

**1** Complete the adjectives for describing food and restaurants with *a, e, i, o* or *u*.

1 n _i_ c _e_

3 g r __ __ t

5 f __ v __ __ r __ t __

2 l __ v __ l y

4 g __ __ d

## Help with Writing

When you write a blog post, you can talk directly to your readers. At the beginning of his post, Luka writes, 'Hi, everyone!' He also asks his readers questions like 'How about egg and banana soup?' Writers of blog posts also use lots of exclamation marks (!) to help their readers understand how strongly they feel about what they are writing.

**2** Imagine you write a blog about food. Write a post about a restaurant or café that you like in your town. Include the following information:

- The name of your blog.
- The name of the restaurant/café.
- The food you can order there.
- Your favourite thing to eat there.
- When or how often you go there.

6TH JANUARY

## Shall we visit _____?

(____ comments) 😊 😐 ☹

_____
_____
_____
_____
_____
_____
_____
_____
_____
_____
_____
_____
_____

# Listening: food and drink

**1** 🎧 **05** Listen and number the pictures.

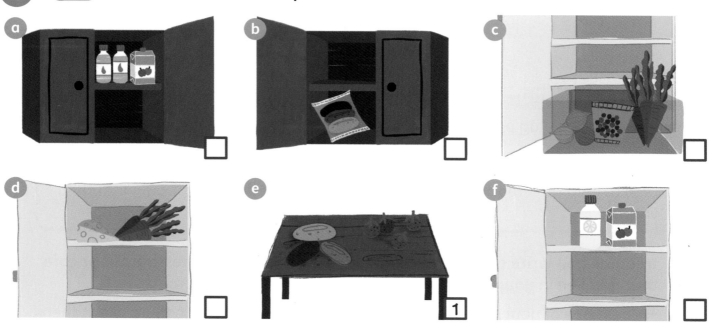

**2** 🎧 **06** Listen and match.

Dad and Vicky

Fred and Daisy

Sally and John

Mum and Jim

**1** Draw five foods in the shopping basket, then say. You can draw more than one piece of each food.

There are two rolls and three carrots in my shopping basket. There is an apple …

**2** Work with a friend. Play the memory game.

There are three carrots in your shopping basket.

That's right!

There is one roll.

That's wrong! There are two rolls.

**3** With your friend, plan your lunch and dinner. Use the ideas from the box and your ideas.

> cheese sandwich   pea soup   pizza   salad
> chicken soup   sausages   fish   tomatoes

Shall we have salad for lunch?

OK. How about some pea soup too?

What time is it, Zoe?

It's **quarter past** four.

**Language focus**

Use these words and phrases to talk about the time:
**o'clock**, **quarter past**, **half past**, **quarter to**.

*It's four **o'clock** (4:00). It's **quarter past** four (4:15).*
*It's **half past** four (4:30). It's **quarter to** five (4:45).*

**1** **What time is it? Look and circle the correct time.**

1 It's quarter past seven. / It's quarter past eight.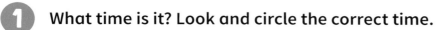

2 It's half past eight. / It's half past nine.

3 It's quarter past five. / It's half past five.

4 It's quarter past seven. / It's quarter to seven.

5 It's half past five. / It's half past six.

6 It's six o'clock. / It's twelve o'clock.

**2** Complete the text with the words from the box.

seven   o'clock   ~~half~~   quarter   past

I've got a dog called Marmalade. I take her for a walk every day at
**(1)** ___half___ past four. We walk along the river in the park next to our
house. We get home at five **(2)** _____. I help Dad cook the dinner and
at **(3)** _____ to six we eat. At half **(4)** _____ six Mum washes up
and I dry the dishes. Do you know what Marmalade does? She waits by the
back door. I say, 'What do you want, Marmalade?' I know what she wants –
another walk! 'We can't go now,' I say. 'It's almost **(5)** _____ o'clock!'

**3** Write the times.

1   __It's quarter past two.__

2   _____

3   _____

4   _____

5   _____

6   _____

# Adverbs for time

My Saturday? Well, I **sometimes** make breakfast for Mum, Dad and my little sisters. Then we all do the shopping – we **always** go to the big supermarket near the park. In the afternoon, I play football or computer games with my friends. I **never** cook the evening meal, but I wash up after dinner. In the evening, I **usually** watch a film with my family. That's my favourite part of the day.

## Language focus

Use **adverbs for time** – **always**, **usually**, **sometimes**, **never** – to talk about how often someone does something.

*My father **always** tidies up after dinner.*

Put the adverb for time before the main verb in a sentence:

|  | **Adverb** | **Main verb** |  |
|---|---|---|---|
| *I* | ***always*** | *get up* | *at six o'clock.* |
| *She* | ***usually*** | *does* | *her homework before dinner.* |
| *He* | ***sometimes*** | *washes up* | *after dinner.* |
| *We* | ***never*** | *do* | *the shopping on Sundays.* |

**1** **Put the adverbs in the right place in the sentences.**

1 I brush my teeth after dinner. (always)

   I always brush my teeth after dinner.

2 My father goes to bed early. (never)

   _____

3 My sister does lots of homework at the weekend. (usually)

   _____

4 My mother does the shopping on Fridays. (sometimes)

   _____

5 My brother goes to bed at ten o'clock. (always)

   _____

**2** Complete the sentences with the correct adverbs.

| | cook | wash up | dry the dishes | feed the cat |
|---|---|---|---|---|
| Me | ✗ | ✗ | ✓ | ✗ |
| Mum | ✓ | ✗ | ✓✓ | ✓✓✓ |
| Dad | ✓ | ✓✓✓ | ✓ | ✗ |
| My brother | ✗ | ✗ | ✓ | ✗ |
| My sister | ✓ | ✗ | ✓ | ✗ |

Always ✓✓✓    Usually ✓✓    Sometimes ✓    Never ✗

1 I _____**never**_____ feed the cat.

2 Mum _____ dries the dishes.

3 Dad _____ washes up.

4 My brother _____ dries the dishes.

5 My sister _____ washes up.

6 My brother _____ feeds the cat.

7 I _____ cook.

**3** Write six more sentences about the family in Activity 2.

1 _____

2 _____

3 _____

4 _____

5 _____

6 _____

# Reading: a newspaper article

**1** Read the newspaper article. Then answer the questions.

## THE DAILY SPECTACLE

31st January

### A VERY BUSY FAMILY

The Sánchez family of Oviedo, Spain, are a very busy family – they don't stop! There are six members of the family: Grandma Sánchez, Mr and Mrs Sánchez, and their children, Pedro, Juan and Gracia. Everyone in the Sánchez family knows what to do and when to do it. Saturday is the busiest day of the week. On Saturday morning, at half past eight, Gracia always sweeps the floors. Juan usually goes with Mr and Mrs Sánchez to the supermarket to do the shopping. At twelve o'clock on Saturday, Pedro cooks lunch for everyone. After lunch, Mr Sánchez washes up and Mrs Sánchez dries the dishes. On Saturday afternoon, Grandma Sánchez and Gracia tidy up the house. On sunny days, Mr and Mrs Sánchez work in the garden. In the evening, Pedro cooks dinner. After dinner, Mrs Sánchez washes up and Mr Sánchez dries the dishes. At nine o'clock, everyone in the Sánchez family tidies their room and then goes to bed. They are all so tired after such a busy day!

1 Who always sweeps the floors?  **Gracia always sweeps the floors.**

2 Who usually does the shopping with Mr and Mrs Sanchez? _____

_____

3 Who cooks lunch and dinner? _____

4 Who washes up after lunch and dinner? _____

_____

5 Who dries the dishes after lunch and dinner? _____

_____

6 What time does everyone go to bed on Saturday evening? _____

_____

**1** **Write sentences about daily tasks so they are true for you.**

1 I always _____.   3 I usually _____.

2 I sometimes _____.   4 I never _____.

## Help with Writing

When you write a newspaper article, tell your readers where, when, why and how something happens. People read newspaper articles for information and they want to learn as much as possible.

**2** **Imagine you write for the newspaper *The Daily Spectacle*. Write an article about one day in the life of a family similar to the Sánchez family. Include the following information:**

- The name of the family.
- How many children there are in the family.
- The daily tasks each member of the family does, when they do them, and how often.

# THE DAILY SPECTACLE

31st January

_____
_____
_____
_____
_____
_____
_____
_____
_____
_____
_____

# Listening: tasks and times

**1** 🎧 **07** **Listen and circle the correct time.**

**1** Ann gets up at …

a  b

**2** Ann has breakfast at …

a  b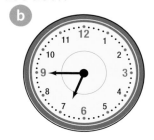

**3** Ann brushes her teeth at …

a  b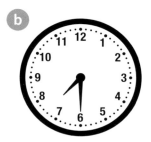

**4** Ann and her brother take their dog for a walk at …

a  b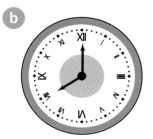

**5** Ann gets back at …

a 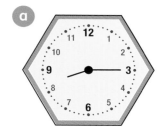 b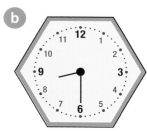

**6** Ann and her brother leave the house at …

a 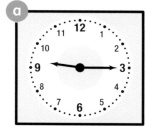 b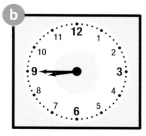

**2** 🎧 **08** **Listen and write *Jane* or *Peter*.**

1 ___**Peter**___ sometimes washes up after dinner.

2 _____ usually dries the dishes.

3 _____ likes cooking on Fridays.

4 _____ always cooks pasta on Sundays.

5 _____ usually helps to tidy up the house at the weekend.

6 _____ doesn't like tidying up.

**1** **Look and write the daily task. Then play the description game.**

> You do this after dinner. You do it in the kitchen.

> Is it 'wash up'?

> That's right!

take the dog for
a walk

_____

_____

_____

_____

_____

_____

_____

_____

_____

_____

**2** **Work with a friend. Talk about the daily tasks in Activity 1.**

> Do you like cooking?

> No, I don't!

> I do! I sometimes make pizza with my mum.

**3** **With your friend, plan your daily tasks for one week. Write them in the diary.**

|  | Me | My friend |
|---|---|---|
| Monday |  |  |
| Tuesday |  |  |
| Wednesday |  |  |
| Thursday |  |  |
| Friday |  |  |

> Do you want to feed the cat on Monday?

> OK. Can you do the washing up?

> Yes, I can.

# 4 Prepositions

Excuse me, can you tell me where the cinema is, please? I can't find it on my map.

Yes, of course! There it is, **opposite** the park, **between** the car park and the funfair.

## Language focus

Use the prepositions **opposite**, **near**, **above**, **between**, **next to**, **in front of** and **below** to say where one thing is in relation to something else. We use prepositions to talk about places, objects and people.

*The school is **next to** the tower.*

**1** **Circle the correct preposition.**

1 The market is *above* / *below* the tower.
2 The sports centre is *opposite* / *next to* the library.
3 The castle is *in front of* / *near* the park.
4 The window is *below* / *above* the clock.
5 The map is *in front of* / *above* the window.

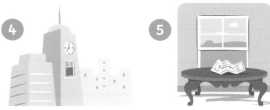

**2** Look at the picture and complete the dialogue with the words from the box.

Opposite   ~~where~~   between   front   near

Hi, Vic. I'm in town, next to the cinema. I'm looking for the new café. Can you tell me **(1)** ___**where**___ it is? I can't find it.

The new café? No problem! Can you see the tower? The new café is **(2)** _____ the tower, in **(3)** _____ of the park.

Oh, I know! It's **(4)** _____ the bus station and the bank.

That's right! **(5)** _____ the market.

Thank you!

**3** Look at the picture again and answer the questions. More than one answer is possible.

1 Where is the bank? __It's near the café. It's opposite the park.__

2 Where is the café? _____

3 Where is the sports centre? _____

4 Where is the cinema? _____

5 Where is the library? _____

6 Where is the bus station? _____

# Be going to + infinitive of purpose

Where are you going, Frank?

**I'm going to** the library to get a book about famous explorers, Dad.

Use **be going to** + **infinitive of purpose** to tell someone where you are going and why you are going there.

Where are you going?    I **am going to** the market **to buy** some fruit and vegetables.

Where is he / she going?    He / she **is going to** the sports centre **to play** table tennis.

Where are we / they going?    We / they **are going to** the café **to have** lunch.

**1** Correct the sentences.

1 She going to the square to meet her family.

   _She's going to the square to meet her family._

2 He's going to the park to playing football.

   _____

3 They're going the bank to get some money.

   _____

4 I'm go to the Soup Shop to have dinner with my parents.

   _____

5 We're going to the sports centre play basketball.

   _____

6 You're going to the café have a glass of lemonade.

   _____

**2** Make sentences using the information in the table.

| I | cinema | buy | bread |
|---|---|---|---|
| You | supermarket | watch | swimming |
| He / She | my cousin's house | help | film |
| We | sports centre | play | in the garden |
| They | my grandparents' house | go | computer games |

1  I'm going to the cinema to watch a film.

2  _____

3  _____

4  _____

5  _____

**3** Write sentences using *going to* + infinitive of purpose.

Today is Saturday. My friends and I are in town. We're all doing different things.

(1) Mandy / go to / square / meet / her cousin.
Mandy's going to the square to meet her cousin.

(2) Richard and Pierre / go to / cinema / watch / new adventure film.

_____

(3) Serge / go to / library / get / books for his Science project.

_____

(4) Martina / go to / market / buy / birthday present for her sister.

_____

(5) Emma / go to / sports centre / go swimming.

_____

(6) We / go to / café / later / drink milkshakes!

_____

# Reading: a postcard

**1** Read the postcard. Write *t* (true) or *f* (false). Correct the false sentences.

Dear Mum and Dad

It's day one of our school trip! What a great place! I'm having a lovely time. Our hotel is opposite a park. The hotel is brilliant! Next to it there is a castle. Near the castle there is an old tower in a square. I want to climb it to see the views of the town. I love it here!

We're going to the museum in the centre to look at the paintings now. They have some by Da Vinci, Rembrandt and Van Gogh! Have to go!

Hope you are well

Love Ali

Mr and Mrs Muhtar

55 East Ninth Street

New York

NY 10011

USA

**1** It's the second week of Ali's school trip.   [f]

**It's the first day of Ali's school trip.**

**2** Ali's hotel is next to a museum.   ☐

**3** The tower isn't a new building.   ☐

**4** Below the tower there is a square.   ☐

**5** There aren't any paintings by famous artists in the museum.   ☐

**1** Complete the phrases with the words from the box.

brilliant   love   having   ~~place~~

1 What a great ___place___ !

2 I'm _____ a lovely time.

3 The hotel is _____ !

4 I _____ it here!

**Help with Writing**

There is not much space to write on a postcard, so sometimes the subject pronoun *I* is missed out. Ali writes 'Have to go' at the end of his postcard instead of 'I have to go'.

**2** Imagine you are on a school trip, staying in a hotel in a city. Write a postcard to your parents. Use Ali's postcard to help you. Include the following information:

• Where you are staying.

• What you are staying near, next to, opposite, etc.

• Where you are going and why you are going there.

# Listening: places in a town

**1** 🎧 **09** **Listen to the children talk about places. Circle the correct answers.**

1 Where does the girl want to go?

   a To the tower.      **b** To the cinema.

2 Where are they going?

   a To the bus station.   b To the park.

3 Where is the funfair?

   a Behind the car park.   b Behind the supermarket.

4 Where is the sports centre?

   a Next to the park.   b Behind the bank.

5 What is opposite the train station?

   a The map of the town.   b The market.

6 What is below the castle?

   a The café.   b The river.

**2** 🎧 **10** **Listen and match.**

Oliver

Dylan

Dad

Holly

Julia

Joe

 **a**

 **b**

 **c**

 **d**

**e**

 **f**

**1** Complete the map of the street with the places from the box. Give your street a name.

tower    bus station    supermarket    library    sports centre    bank

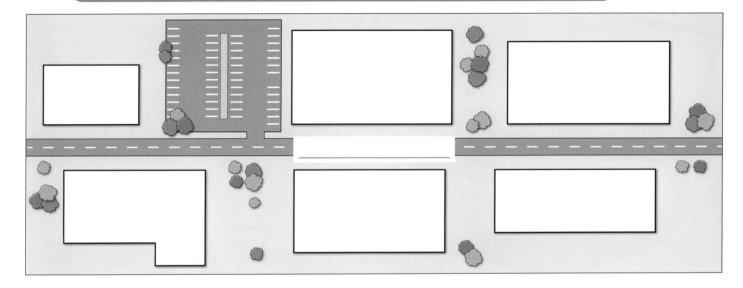

## Help with Speaking

When you speak, there can be words that are difficult to say in English. Ask your teacher for help. Then you can practise saying the difficult words with a friend.

**2** Work with a friend. Talk about your street map in Activity 1.

> What's the name of your street?

> It's Spider Street.

> Where is the supermarket?

> It's opposite the sports centre, next to the bus station.

**3** Where are you going? Ask and answer. Use your map in Activity 1.

> Hi, Sophie! Where are you going?

> Hello, Max. I'm going to the sports centre to play football.

> Have a great time!

# 5 Was / Were

Hi, Uncle Mike
Yesterday **was** great! We **were** at Nathan's
ninth birthday party. Everyone **was** there.
There **were** balloons and games. There
**was** a really big cake, too! How are you?
Do you like living by the sea in Vancouver?
We all want to visit you there soon!
Love, Sally

**Language focus**

**Was** / **Were** are the positive past simple forms of **be**. **Wasn't** / **Weren't** are
the negative past simple forms of **be**. Use **was** / **were** / **wasn't** / **weren't**
to talk about:

**places:**     We **were** on the beach.

**feelings:**  Mum **was** tired.

**people:**    My aunt **was** a film star.
                    I / He / She **was** / **wasn't** hot yesterday.
                    You / We / They **were** / **weren't** in the park all day.

**1**  **Put the sentences into the past. Use** *was / were.*

1  There is a small shark, too!  There was a small shark, too!

2  I'm scared! _____

3  We're at the beach. _____

4  There are dolphins, seals and turtles in the sea. _____

5  It's hot. _____

6  I'm in the sea in my new swimsuit. _____

**2** Make your answers in Activity 1 negative.

1 <u>There wasn't a small shark.</u>

2 _____

3 _____

4 _____

5 _____

6 _____

**3** Order the sentences in Activity 1 to make a story. More than one order is possible.

1 _____

2 _____

3 _____

4 _____

5 _____

6 _____

**4** Complete the text with *was, were, wasn't* or *weren't*.

Yesterday (1) ___**was**___ a busy day!
We (2) _____ in the park in the
morning. There (3) _____ a football
match, but there (4) _____ many
goals. Only one! In the afternoon we
(5) _____ at my cousin's house. There
(6) _____ cheese sandwiches, but there
(7) _____ any cake this time. In the
evening we (8) _____ at the cinema
to see that new film about life under the
sea. It (9) _____ very interesting!
(10) We _____ all very tired at the end of the day.

# Questions and answers with was / were

**Were** you at the beach?

Yes, we **were**, Gran! It was great!

## Language focus

Put **was** / **were** at the beginning of the sentence to make a Yes/No question.

**Was** Hector in the park?   *Yes, he* **was**, *with his new kite!*

**Were** *you … ?*   *Yes, I* **was**.

*No, I* **wasn't**.

**Were** *we / they … ?*   *Yes, we / they* **were**.   **Was** *he / she … ?*   *Yes, he / she* **was**.

*No, we / they* **weren't**.   *No, he / she* **wasn't**.

Use a question word such as **where** to ask a different type of question with **was** / **were**.

**Where** *were you?*   *I* **was** *at home.*

**Where** *was Harriet?*   *She* **was** *at the swimming pool.*

---

**1**  Complete the mini-dialogues with *was, were, wasn't* or *weren't*.

1  'Where ___**was**___ Anne yesterday?' 'She _____ at the park with her friends.'

2  '_____ Ed at school last week?' 'No, he _____. He _____ at home because he was unwell.'

3  '_____ my keys on the table?' 'No, they _____.'

4  '_____ Sylvia at the birthday party?' 'Yes, she _____. She was very happy.'

5  '_____ your friends on the beach?' 'No, they _____. It was too cold.'

6  'Where _____ Joe and Bill on Saturday afternoon?' 'I think they _____ at the cinema.'

**2** **Match the questions with the answers.**

1 Was Jack at the swimming pool?

2 Were your brother and sister at the beach at the weekend?

3 Where were you on Sunday, Louise?

4 Were your grandparents in the garden, Liz?

5 Were there seahorses and starfish in the sea?

6 Was there a clock on the tower in the square?

a No, they weren't. It was too hot to do gardening.

b I was at home all day. I was tired.

c Yes, there was. A very old one.

d Yes, they were. They were in the sea too.

e No, he wasn't. It wasn't open.

f Yes, there were! Lots of them. They were beautiful!

**3** **Look at the pictures and answer the questions.**

1 Was Mina in a boat? **Yes, she was.** _____

2 Were Bryan and Johanna in school? _____

3 Was Samantha at the museum? _____

4 Was Damian at the sports centre? _____

5 Was Stefanie in bed? _____

6 Were the children at the beach? _____

# Reading: a factual description

**1**  **Read the text. Circle the correct answers.**

## The MEGALODON

There were once many different animals in the water from the ones we see today. There were sea birds called great auks and there were baiji: Chinese river dolphins. Another animal, now extinct, was the megalodon. Megalodons were huge sharks between 14 and 18 metres long. Their teeth were 21 centimetres long! These enormous creatures were very fast swimmers and were in the waters around Europe, Africa and North and South America between 16.1 and 1.6 million years ago. They were meat eaters and their favourite food was whales and seals.

1 Extinct animals are ones that *live / do not live* now.
2 Megalodons were *dolphins / sharks.*
3 Megalodons were very *big / small.*
4 Megalodons were *slow / fast.*
5 Megalodons were in *many different places / only one place.*

**1** **Complete the fact file with the words from the box.**

75–65 million years ago    ~~archelon~~    4.6 metres    fish and plants    the open sea

## FACT FILE

Name: _____archelon_____
Size: _____
Place: _____
Time: _____
Food: _____

### Help with Writing

We read factual descriptions when we want to find out something really interesting about a subject. For example, in the description of the megalodon we learn that its teeth were 21 centimetres long. When you write a factual description, include information to make your readers say, 'Wow!'

**2** **Write a factual description of the archelon. Use the information in the fact file and the description of the megalodon to help you.**

Archelon
The archelon was a giant turtle.
_____
_____
_____
_____
_____
_____
_____

# Listening: sea creatures

**1** 🎧 11 Listen and tick ☑ the sea creatures at the Sea Life Centre.

**2** 🎧 12 Listen and draw lines.

Leo　　　George　　　Amy　　　Penny　　　Eva　　　Paul

**1** Imagine you were in the sea yesterday. What was there? Draw five animals and say.

> There were two big dolphins. There was a small shark. There were …

**2** Work with a friend. Play the memory game.

> There were two dolphins in the sea.

> That's right!

> Was there a turtle?

> No, there wasn't.

**3** Think of a place and imagine you were there at the weekend. Talk about your place. Can your friend guess it?

> Who was with you?

> What wasn't there?

> What was there?

> I was at a fantastic place at the weekend. I was there with my parents and cousins. There were some amazing animals. There were some lions and … There weren't any …

> Were you at a wildlife park?

> Yes, I was!

# 6 Comparatives

**Excuse me. How much are those laptops?**

£450

£699

**Well, this one is cheaper than that one. This one is £450 and that one is £699.**

## Language focus

Use **comparatives** to compare two people, places or things.

*The doctor is **taller than** Ewan.*

There are some rules to learn:

Add **er** to the end of adjectives with one syllable: *slow / slower*

Put **more** before adjectives of three or more syllables: *difficult / more difficult*

Sometimes, when an adjective is written **consonant** + **vowel** + **consonant**, double the final consonant: *sad / sadder*

When an adjective ends in **y**, change the **y** to an **i** and add **er**: *busy / busier*

There are some irregular adjectives that do not follow rules:
*good    better        bad    worse*

---

**1** Write the comparatives.

1 small _____smaller_____

2 fast _____

3 new _____

4 quiet _____

5 big _____

6 happy _____

7 funny _____

8 famous _____

9 beautiful _____

10 expensive _____

**2** Use the comparatives from Activity 1 and write sentences.

1  The yellow car is slower
than the black car. (slow)

2  _____
_____ (big)

the new tower    the old tower

Clock A    Clock B

3  _____
_____ (tall)

4  _____
_____ (old)

SP Mini    Com20 Plus

5  _____
_____ (cheap)

6  _____
_____ (sad)

**3** Complete the dialogue with the words from the box.

smaller   cheaper   bigger than   better   more   ~~expensive~~

| Katya | How much is this mobile phone? |
| Shop assistant | Oh, that one is £399. |
| Katya | That's too (1) __expensive__ . I'd like a (2) _____ one. |
| Shop assistant | This one is £200. |
| Katya | That's a (3) _____ price. |
| Shop assistant | As you can see, it's much (4) _____ our other phones, and it's got a (5) _____ beautiful design. |
| Katya | I like it, but it's too big for me. Have you got any (6) _____ phones? |

# Superlatives

Who's **the oldest** in your ice-skating team, Ronnie?

Shaun. He's 11.

Language focus

**Superlatives** are used to describe a quality that a thing or person has the most or least of in a group.

*Laila is **the cleverest** student in the class.*

There are some rules to learn:

Put **the** before the adjective and add **est** to the end of adjectives with one syllable: *slow / **the slowest***

Put **the most** before adjectives of three or more syllables: ***difficult / the most difficult***

Sometimes, when an adjective is written **consonant** + **vowel** + **consonant**, double the final consonant: *sad / **the saddest***

When an adjective ends in **y**, change the **y** to an **i** and add **est**: *busy / **the busiest***

**1** Write the superlatives.

1 small ___the smallest___

2 fast _____

3 new _____

4 quiet _____

5 big _____

6 happy _____

7 funny _____

8 famous _____

9 beautiful _____

10 expensive _____

**2** Complete the poem with superlatives from Activity 1.

Jack can run. He can run very fast.
He's (1) __the fastest__ boy in school,

And Jane tells jokes like no one else.
She's (2) _____ and she's cool.

Robert's (3) _____ – a friendly boy.
He laughs and smiles all day,

While Sally's (4) _____. She doesn't
speak up. She says she's got nothing
to say.

(5) _____ student in our year is
Beth McBeth – she's with me.

I'm going to tell her everything and
introduce class 6C.

**3** Answer the questions. Write complete sentences.

1 Who is the funniest person in your class?

_____

2 Who is the oldest person in your class?

_____

3 Who is the youngest person in your class?

_____

4 Who is the best at drawing in your class?

_____

5 Who is the cleverest person in your class?

_____

# Reading: an advertisement

**1** Look at the information in the advert. Then complete the sentences.

Do you need to go shopping for a new toothbrush? If you want a brighter smile than anyone else's, you need

The Tooth Company's

# Pearly White X300

– the electric toothbrush that gives you the cleanest teeth in the world!

The Pearly White X100 was good.

The Pearly White X200 was better.

The Pearly White X300 is the **best**.

The Pearly White X300 comes with its own beautiful carrying case at no extra cost! Buy it today to take advantage of our special price!

**Was £89.99, now only £69.99!**

Available in all good electrical shops or at
**www.thetoothcompany.com**

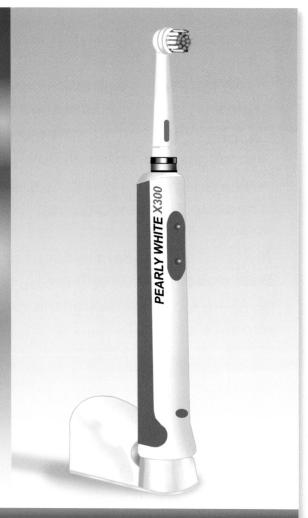

PEARLY WHITE X300

1 The Tooth Company says the Pearly White X300 gives people the
   __cleanest__ teeth.

2 The advert says the Pearly White X200 was _____ than the Pearly White X100.

3 The advert says the Pearly White X300 is the Tooth Company's _____ toothbrush.

4 The Pearly White X300 is 20 pounds _____ than it was before.

5 The Pearly White X300 gives you a _____ smile.

**1** **Write the words underneath the pictures.**

> laptop   games console   ~~tablet~~   mobile phone

1 __tablet__     2 _____     3 _____     4 _____

## Help with Writing

Advertisements often use comparatives and superlatives to try to make people buy products. Look at the example of the Tooth Company's advert for the Pearly White X300. It says the toothbrush is 'the best'.

**2** **Imagine you work for one of the following:**

- The Tablet Shop.
- Laptops Incorporated.
- The Mobile Phone Emporium.
- Games Console World.

Write an advertisement for a laptop, games console, tablet or mobile phone. Give your product a name and a price. Try to use comparatives and superlatives when describing it. Use the Tooth Company's advertisement to help you write yours.

_____

_____

_____

_____

_____

_____

_____

# Listening: technology

**1** 🎧 **13** Listen and number the photos.

a

b

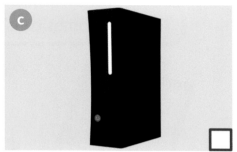
c

d  1

e

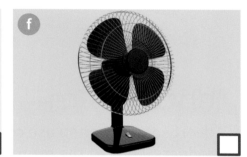
f

**2** 🎧 **14** Listen. Are sentences 1–6 true or false?

1 Sam's laptop is bigger than Suzie's.   **f**

2 The red clock is the most beautiful. ☐

3 The green mobile phone is the most expensive. ☐

4 The black torch is smaller than the brown torch. ☐

5 The orange walkie-talkie is the cheapest in the shop. ☐

6 Gwen's games console is faster than Jon's. ☐

**1** **Talk about the mobile phones. Use the words from the box.**

Which phone is the biggest?

The Tech 300!

| biggest   smallest   shortest   longest   nicest   ugliest   cheapest   most expensive |

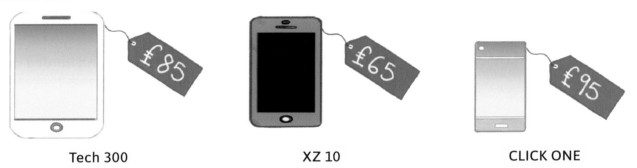

£85

Tech 300

£65

XZ 10

£95

CLICK ONE

**2** **Draw a special mobile phone. Complete and practise.**

This is a special mobile phone.
It's called _____ .
You can _____ and
it _____ . It's the
_____ mobile phone
in the world!

**3** **Talk about your special mobile phone.**

HELLO!

This is a special mobile phone. It's called the Talk 24. You can talk to it and it talks to you. It's the funniest mobile phone in the world!

# 7 Past simple: regular verbs

> I **jumped** up to catch the ball, but I **tripped** and **landed** on my arm.

**Language focus**

Use the **past simple** to talk about something that happened in the past at a specific time.

*She **played** football yesterday.*

Regular verbs in the past simple are verbs which end in **ed**, such as **played**, **watched** and **visited**. They are the same for every person: **I**, **you**, **he**, **she**, **we**, **they**.

**1** Put the verbs into the past simple.

---

To: Jen

From: Marco

---

*Hi, Jen*

*Is your arm better? I hope so. Last week was the half-term holiday. No school – brilliant! On Monday, I (1) __played__ (play) basketball with my cousins. What a game! On Tuesday, Fabio and I (2) _____ (watch) a film at the new cinema in town. It was boring. On Wednesday, my sister and I (3) _____ (visit) my grandmother. We (4) _____ (walk) around the beautiful park next to her house. On Thursday, I (5) _____ (cook) the evening meal for everyone – spaghetti! I love cooking. On Friday, I (6) _____ (stay) at home because I was a bit tired. At the weekend, it was really sunny. I (7) _____ (help) my parents in the garden. I really (8) _____ (like) my half-term holiday! How was your week, Jen?*

*Write soon!*

*Marco*

**2** What did the Keita family do on Saturday? Complete the sentences with the words from the box in the correct form. Then match the sentences with the pictures.

land   look   shout   watch   ~~play~~   talk

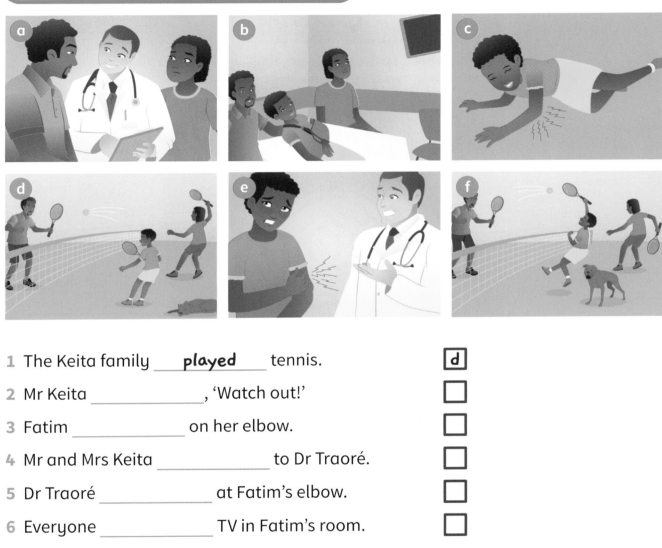

1 The Keita family _____**played**_____ tennis.   [d]

2 Mr Keita _____, 'Watch out!'   ☐

3 Fatim _____ on her elbow.   ☐

4 Mr and Mrs Keita _____ to Dr Traoré.   ☐

5 Dr Traoré _____ at Fatim's elbow.   ☐

6 Everyone _____ TV in Fatim's room.   ☐

**3** What did your family do at the weekend? Write sentences in the past simple using these verbs: *play, watch, listen to, cook, help, visit.*

1 _____

2 _____

3 _____

4 _____

5 _____

6 _____

# Past simple: irregular verbs

You **weren't** at school yesterday.

No, I **had** earache. I **felt** awful.

**Language focus**

**Irregular verbs in the past simple** do not end in **ed**.

*Alison **came** home by train.*

The past simple of **come** is **came** not **comed**. Irregular verbs in the past simple have forms that you have to learn, but the forms are the same for every person: **I**, **you**, **he**, **she**, **we**, **they**.

**1** Put the verbs in 1–9 into the past simple.

1 wake up __woke up__     4 have _____     7 say _____

2 give _____     5 go _____     8 write _____

3 feel _____     6 eat _____     9 see _____

**2** Complete the blog with the past simple form of the verbs from Activity 1.
Use each verb only once.

## Joan's Health Blog

I **(1)** <u>woke up</u> early. I was very excited. I **(2)** _____ to the hospital on the bus.
The hospital? Yes, that's right! I was OK, but it was a very special day for me. I want
to be a doctor like Olivia's dad. Dr Mathews **(3)** _____, 'Come to the hospital
for a day, Joan.' It was brilliant! I **(4)** _____ nervous,
but Dr Mathews was great. He **(5)** _____
me a tour of the wards. I **(6)** _____ the
special machines and met the nurses.
They worked really hard. At lunchtime,
I **(7)** _____ my sandwiches in the
canteen with all the doctors. I asked the
doctors lots of questions! I **(8)** _____
a great time! When I got home I
**(9)** _____ an email to Dr Mathews
to say thank you!

**3** There are eight mistakes with past simple verbs in the text. The first one is given.
Can you find the other seven?

Last week (is) a difficult week. Everyone was sick. Vicky had toothache, Martin
had a cold and I have a terrible cough. I wake up with it on Monday morning.
'Oh no,' I say to Mum and Dad. 'I've got another cough.' I go to the doctor
and he give me some special medicine. Vicky and Martin had pills to take
too. We are all OK by the end of the week, but Mum and Dad feel very tired.

| 1 | <u>was</u> | 4 | _____ | 7 | _____ |
| 2 | _____ | 5 | _____ | 8 | _____ |
| 3 | _____ | 6 | _____ | | |

# Reading: a story

**1** Read the story. Put the events in order.

## The Girl Who Needed A Break

What an awful Monday! One of the worst. Sally was at her friend's house to do some homework. 'What can I do, Mira?' Sally said. 'I felt awful last week. I felt awful yesterday. I feel awful today. I've got this awful cough, Mira. And this awful cold. And this awful headache. And this awful earache. And this awful stomach-ache. Really, I feel quite awful.'

Mira looked at Sally and smiled. 'Sally,' Mira said, 'there is nothing wrong with you! There was nothing wrong with you last week. There was nothing wrong with you yesterday. There is nothing wrong with you today.'

'Um, I don't understand. What do you mean?'

Mira smiled again. 'Sally,' Mira said, 'you're tired! That's all. You worked very hard last week. You worked very hard yesterday. You worked very hard today. You always work very hard, Sally. You're the best student in the school.'

'I try hard. That's all.'

'But there is something you're not very good at.'

'Really?' Sally wanted to be good at everything. 'What's that?'

'The most important part of studying hard is *not* studying hard. You need to take breaks, Sally. You need a rest.'

'A rest!' Sally said. 'A rest, Mira? But I can't have rests! I've got too many exams to study for. I've got to learn all about the Incas of Peru and food chains in rainforests and how people feel when they have a fever. I can't have a rest. Let's not talk about breaks or rests. What I need is something for this awful cough, and this awful cold, and this awful headache, and this awful earache, and this awful …'

a Mira tells Sally that she needs a rest.  ☐

b Mira says that Sally is not unwell.  ☐

c Sally says that she doesn't understand.  ☐

d Sally says that she is unwell.  [1]

e Mira tells Sally that she is very tired.  ☐

f Sally tells Mira that she has to study for her exams.  ☐

**1** Complete the table with the information from the box.

> Sally, Mira    Mira's house    Monday    ~~The Girl Who Needed A Break~~
> Sally says she is unwell but Mira says she is OK.

| The title (what the story is called) | The Girl Who Needed A Break |
|---|---|
| The characters (the people in the story) | |
| The plot (what happens in the story) | |
| The setting (the place where the story happens) | |
| The time frame (when the story happens) | |

**2** You are going to write a short story in the past simple. Before you write your story, plan it by making notes about:

- The title.
- The characters.
- The plot.
- The setting.
- The time frame.

**3** Now write your short story. Use the story of Sally and your notes from Activity 2 to help you.

_____
_____
_____
_____
_____

**Help with Writing**

Writing stories is all about making something interesting for the reader. Writers try to catch the attention of their readers immediately, from the very first sentence. Try to write a first sentence that makes a reader want to read the rest of the story!

# Listening: health

**1** 🎧 **15** Listen and tick ✓ Nick's health problems.

1. □
2. □
3. □
4. □
5. □
6. □

**2** 🎧 **16** Listen and put Kate's story in order.

- □ Kate played football and she was the goalkeeper.
- □ Kate and her sister played computer games.
- □ Thomas kicked the ball at Kate.
- 1 Last Saturday, Kate went to the park with her friends.
- □ Kate got the ball, but she hurt her knee.
- □ At home, Kate watched a football match with her parents.

## 1 What's the matter? Choose, say and guess.

What's the matter?

I've got problem number 4.

You've got a stomach-ache.

## 2 Work with a friend. Talk about the health problems in Activity 1. Use the ideas from the box and your ideas.

stay at home    go to the doctor's    take some medicine
sleep    get some fresh air    have a hot drink    put some ice on it
have a rest    drink lots of water    take a pill

I had a headache at the weekend.

Oh, poor you!

I stayed at home and had a rest.

### Help with Speaking

A story has got a beginning, a middle and an end. These parts help us understand what is happening. Before you tell a story, think about its three parts. What do you want to say in each one?

## 3 With your friend, tell the story about Hugo. You can use the verbs from the box in the past simple.

go    hurt    sit    put
give    have    watch    feel

Last Sunday, Hugo went to the park to run. He was …

# 8 Negatives with past simple

We went to a pizza restaurant on the last night of our trip. It was Leah's birthday. I **didn't like** my pizza. It was horrible!

**Language focus**

**Negatives with past simple** are formed with **did** + **not** + **infinitive**.

*Carla **didn't go** to the party because she had lots of homework.*

The forms are the same for every person: **I**, **you**, **he**, **she**, **we**, **they**.

**1** Complete the sentences with the verbs from the box in the negative form of the past simple.

> eat   swim   speak   drink   spend   ~~go~~

I had a great time with my family in Spain because …

1 I ____didn't go____ to bed too late. I got a good night's sleep every night.

2 I _____ too much food. I ate just the right amount.

3 I _____ sugary drinks. I drank water instead.

4 I _____ in the sea in the hottest part of the day. I went in the morning before it got too hot.

5 I _____ lots of money on silly souvenirs. I saved my money for a beautiful book.

6 I _____ English all the time. I learned some Spanish so I could make friends with people.

**2** Put the past simple verbs into the negative form.

## Can I tell you about our trip around the world?

(1) We travelled to so many countries. __We didn't travel to so many countries.__

(2) We saw the Taj Majal in India. _____

(3) We ate tapas in Spain. _____

(4) We walked in the Outback in Australia. _____

(5) We had a great time! _____

(6) We flew to Brazil for the Rio Carnival. _____

(7) We drove to Argentina to see Buenos Aires.

_____

(8) We liked it there. _____

(9) In China, we took photographs of the Great Wall.

_____

(10) In Turkey, we loved the cities of Istanbul and Izmir.

_____

I can't wait for our next adventure. We're going to Egypt!

**3** Match the sentence halves.

1 We went to the cinema to see a new film

2 Mick and Andy had a great time in Germany

3 I went to the park with my friends on Sunday

4 My brother went to Chile last summer

5 I sent postcards home from our trip

6 My sisters stayed in a hotel near the beach

a but I didn't play football. It was too hot for me.

b but I didn't send one to Grandma. I forgot! She wasn't happy with me.

c but they didn't like it very much. They said it was too noisy at night!

d but Mo didn't like it. 'I don't like fantasy films,' he said.

e but he didn't visit the capital, Santiago. He stayed in a place called Valparaíso.

f but they didn't have good weather there. They said it rained almost every day!

**Did** you **have** fun in Cairo, Maya?

Yes, I **did**. It was great, thanks!

## Past simple questions and answers

**Language focus**

**Questions and answers with past simple** are formed with **did** + **infinitive** and **did** (+ **not**) + **infinitive**.

***Did*** you ***go*** *shopping with Tina on Saturday? No, I **didn't**. I was at the gym.*

The forms are the same for every person: **I**, **you**, **he**, **she**, **we**, **they**.

Question words – **why**, **when**, **where**, etc. – go before **did** in the question.

***Where did*** *you go at the weekend?*          *We went to the theatre to see my favourite pop star in concert.*

**1** What did you do at the weekend? Complete the questions with the verbs *play, go, meet* and *read.* Then answer them with *Yes, I did* or *No, I didn't.*

1 Did you ____**go**____ swimming? _____

2 Did you _____ your friends? _____

3 Did you _____ football in the park? _____

4 Did you _____ shopping? _____

5 Did you _____ computer games? _____

6 Did you _____ a book? _____

**2**  Make questions using the information in the table.

| 1 ~~Where~~ | | | stay? (x2) |
| 2 How | | | ~~go?~~ |
| 3 Who | did | you | do? |
| 4 Where | | | go with? |
| 5 What | | | travel there? |
| 6 How long | | | |

1  **Where did you go?**

2  _____

3  _____

4  _____

5  _____

6  _____

**3**  Answer the questions from Activity 2 about the last holiday you went on.

**My last holiday**

1  _____

2  _____

3  _____

4  _____

5  _____

6  _____

**4**  Complete the dialogue with the words from the box.

stay   long   went   ~~Did~~   see

**Tilly**  Hi. How was Sydney? (1) ____**Did**____ you have a good time? What did you (2) _____? How (3) _____ did you stay there?

**Callum**  For three weeks.

**Tilly**  Did you (4) _____ in the city the whole time?

**Callum**  Whoa! What a lot of questions! We (5) _____ to the Gold Coast for a week. It was great!

# Reading: a biography

**1** Read the biography. Then answer the questions.

## The Traveller of the Medieval World

Ibn Battuta was one of the world's greatest travellers. He was born in 1304 in Tangier in Morocco, North Africa, and went to school there. In 1325, he began his travels, going first to Mecca, an important city in modern-day Saudia Arabia. He later decided that he wanted to travel to as many places as possible. He went on to Egypt, China and Tanzania, and to famous cities such as Baghdad and Constantinople, which today is called Istanbul.

For almost 30 years, Ibn Battuta travelled the medieval world, visiting three continents and 40 countries, travelling around 120,000 km. He enjoyed learning about other cultures and met many important people such as the rulers of the countries he visited.

Ibn Battuta wrote a book about his experiences. He called it *Rihla*. This is a word in Classical Arabic that means 'journey'.

We don't know exactly when Ibn Battuta died. Some believe it was in 1368 or 1369. Others say it was in 1377. What we do know of him is that he was one of the world's greatest travellers.

1 What was his name? **Ibn Battuta** _____

2 Where was he born? _____

3 When was he born? _____

4 How many countries did he travel to? _____

5 How many years did he travel for? _____

6 What was he most famous for? _____

7 When did he die? _____

**1** Answer the questions about Nellie Bly with the facts from the box.

> She was a journalist ~~In 1864 in Pennsylvania, USA~~ In 1922 72 days
> Around the world In 1899 By ship, horse and other types of transport

1 Where and when was she born? __In 1864 in Pennsylvania, USA__

2 What was her job? _____

3 Where did she travel? _____

4 How many days did she travel for? _____

5 How did she travel? _____

6 When did she go on the trip? _____

7 When did she die? _____

## Help with Writing

Biographies give us the facts of someone's life – where they were born, where they lived, etc. But a biography can also give the reader more interesting information than that. For example, from the biography of Ibn Battuta, you learned that he spent almost 30 years of his life travelling. In a biography, try to include a really interesting fact about the person.

**2** You are going to write a biography of Nellie Bly. Use the biography of Ibn Battuta and the facts from Activity 1 to help you.

A Biography of Nellie Bly

_____
_____
_____
_____
_____
_____
_____

# Listening: travelling

**1** 🎧 **17** **Listen and match.**

1 Vicky [ a ]

2 Karl [ ]

3 Liz [ ]

4 Tony [ ]

5 Meg [ ]

6 Simon [ ]

Rio de Janeiro, Brazil

Istanbul, Turkey

Buenos Aires, Argentina

Cairo, Egypt

Beijing, China

Madrid, Spain

**2** 🎧 **18** **Listen to Grandpa Joe talk about his trip. Circle the correct answers.**

| | | |
|---|---|---|
| 1 Which country did Grandpa Joe visit? | ⓐ India. | **b** Mexico. |
| 2 How did he travel around there? | **a** By bus and car. | **b** By bus, car and plane. |
| 3 Who did he travel with? | **a** A group of people. | **b** His family. |
| 4 Where did he stay? | **a** In big hotels. | **b** In small hotels. |
| 5 How long did he stay in that country? | **a** One month. | **b** Two weeks. |
| 6 Who wants to visit Australia? | **a** Mary. | **b** Grandpa Joe. |

**1**   **Look at these holiday places. Play the guessing game.**

> Did you swim in the sea?

> No, I didn't.

> Did you go skiing?

> Yes, I did!

> You went to the mountains!

the beach

the mountains

the countryside

a big city

the desert

the forest

**2**   **Think of a trip that you enjoyed. Write answers. Then practise.**

1 Where did you go? _____

2 Who did you go with? _____

3 How did you travel there? _____

4 What did you do and see? _____

5 What was your favourite thing or place? _____

**3**   **Talk about your trip.**

> Last summer, I went to Australia with my mum, dad and sister. We travelled by plane. I swam in the sea over the Great Barrier Reef and saw lots of cool animals. My favourite place was Uluru, a big rock in the desert.

# 9 Future with *be going to* + infinitive

We've all got lots of plans for the summer, Grandpa! Edith**'s going to** travel to Australia with her parents. Nora and Stefan **are going to** stay at a football camp in Poland. And we**'re going to** Japan next week. I can't wait!

## Language focus

Use **future** with **be going to** + **infinitive** for plans and predictions.

*We**'re going to have** a picnic at the weekend. It**'s not going to rain**.*

### Plans

*I**'m not going to stay** at home at the weekend. I**'m going to visit** my cousin.*

*We**'re going to practise** the new dance for the party.*

### Predictions

*I think it**'s going to be** sunny tomorrow.*

*Dad says it**'s going to be** really windy tonight.*

---

**1**    Write sentences with *be going to* + infinitive.

Good morning, everyone. Here is your weather forecast for this week. Today (1) *it / go / to be / very sunny.* Use sun cream! But tomorrow (2) *it / go / to be / different.* (3) *It / go / to rain / all day.* So you'll need your umbrella, your raincoat and your waterproof boots. On Wednesday and Thursday (4) *it / go / to be / cloudy and windy,* but (5) *it / not / go / to rain.* On Friday (6) *we / go / to have / a thunderstorm.* Be careful! That's your forecast. See you next time!

1   <u>It's going to be very sunny.</u>      4   _____

2   _____      5   _____

3   _____      6   _____

**2** Next week, the Sunay family are going on holiday. What are their plans?

1 Mrs Sunay *is not going to send* any emails.

Mrs Sunay _____ books.

2 Mr Sunay _____ any cooking.

Mr Sunay _____ in restaurants.

3 Bebee the dog _____ on the beach.

Bebee the dog _____ for a walk in the rain.

4 Grandpa Sunay

_____ the bathroom.

Grandpa Sunay

_____ on the beach with Grandma Sunay.

**3** Complete the poem with the words from the box.

swim   do   fly   ride   going   We   great   ~~to~~

## The Plan Poem

I'm going to dance, I'm going **(1)** ___**to**___ sing,
I'm going to **(2)** _____ almost everything.
On my trip to the sun with Jane and Mike,
I'm going to swim and **(3)** _____ my bike.
We're **(4)** _____ to go next week by plane, can't wait,
**(5)** _____'re going to go next week, can't be late.
We're going to **(6)** _____ to Spain by plane,
We're going to fly – I can explain.
We're going to **(7)** _____ in the clear blue sea,
It's going to be **(8)** _____ – please come with me!

# Questions and answers with *be going to* + infinitive

**Are** we **going to** make pancakes later?

Yes, we are! It's Pancake Day!

**Language focus**

Put **be** in the correct form at the beginning of the sentence to make a Yes/No question with **be going to** + **infinitive**.

***Are*** *you **going to clean** your bike today? Yes, I am, Mum.*

Question words – **why**, **when**, **where**, etc. – go before **be** in the question.

***What are*** *you **going to do** tonight, Lizzie? I**'m going to go** roller skating!*

**1** Match the questions with the answers.

1 Are you going to go to the concert?
2 What are you going to do on Sunday?
3 Is Maria going to go on holiday this summer?
4 Are you going to play computer games tonight?
5 Who's going to come to the party?
6 Is Hassan going to come back next week?

a Nothing much.
b Yes, I am! I've bought a new one.
c Everyone! It's going to be great!
d Yes, he is. On Monday.
e Yes, she is. To Chile, I think.
f Yes, I am. I can't wait!

**2** Complete the questions with the words from the box.

Who ~~Where~~ When Are Is What

1 __Where__ are you going on holiday?

2 _____ are you going to do?

3 _____ are you going to go with?

4 _____ your brother going to go?

5 _____ you going to go swimming every day?

6 _____ are you going to come back?

**3** The four Baker brothers are going on holiday next week. What are they going to do? Look at the table and answer the questions.

|  | swim | read books | play football | eat ice cream | visit museums |
|---|---|---|---|---|---|
| Peter | ✗ | ✓ | ✗ | ✓ | ✓ |
| Keith | ✓ | ✓ | ✓ | ✓ | ✓ |
| George | ✓ | ✓ | ✗ | ✓ | ✓ |
| Carlos | ✓ | ✗ | ✗ | ✗ | ✓ |

1 Who is going to play football? __Keith is going to play football.__

2 Who is going to do everything? _____

3 Who isn't going to read books? _____

4 What activity is everyone going to do? _____

5 Is Carlos going to play football? _____

6 Is Peter going to read books? _____

7 Are George and Peter going to eat ice cream? _____

8 Is Peter going to swim? _____

**1** Read the letter. Then match the days with the activities.

Office of the Principal
Warsaw School of English
7 Marie Curie Street

Tel: 786 222                                                    18th March

Dear students
We are all very excited about the school trip to Athens on Monday 1st April. We are going to meet at the entrance to Chopin Airport at eight o'clock. The flight leaves at 11 o'clock. We are going to stay in a hostel in the centre of the city. We are going to stay there for four days. This gives us enough time to see Athens.

On Tuesday 2nd, we are going to go to the Parthenon. From the top, there are beautiful views of Athens. It is the perfect place for taking photographs.

On Wednesday 3rd, we are going to take the funicular and go to the top of Mount Lycabettus. On a sunny day you can see all the way to the Aegean Sea.

On Thursday 4th, we are going to spend the day visiting the Plaka District. This is one of the oldest parts of the city. It is very colourful and a good place to do some shopping.

We are going to fly home on the evening of Friday 5th. In the day we are going to the National Archaeological Museum. There you can learn all about ancient Greek art.

If you would like further information about the trip, do not hesitate to call me in my office between 9 a.m. and 5 p.m., Monday to Friday.

Best wishes,
Sebastian Kowalski, principal

1 Monday          a visit the National Archaeological Museum
2 Tuesday         b enjoy the Plaka District
3 Wednesday       c go to the Parthenon
4 Thursday        d meet at the airport
5 Friday          e go to Mount Lycabettus

**1** **Think about your country. Answer the questions.**

1 What are its biggest cities? _____

2 What places are popular with tourists? _____

3 When is the weather good? _____

4 Who are the most famous people of the past from your country?

_____

**2** **Imagine you are the principal of a school. You are going to write a letter telling students about a school trip to a city in your country. Plan the letter by making notes about the following:**

- When visitors are going to go.
- Where visitors are going to go.
- What the weather will be like.

- What visitors are going to do.
- Where visitors are going to stay.
- How long visitors are going to stay.

**Help with Writing**

When writing formal letters, try not to use contractions. Notice that the writer of the letter uses *We are all very excited* instead of *We're all very excited*.

**3** **Now write your letter. Use the letter about Athens and your notes from Activity 2 to help you write.**

Dear students

_____

_____

_____

_____

_____

Best wishes,

_____

# Listening: the weather and holidays

**1** 🎧 **19** Listen and write letters a–f on Finn's diary page.

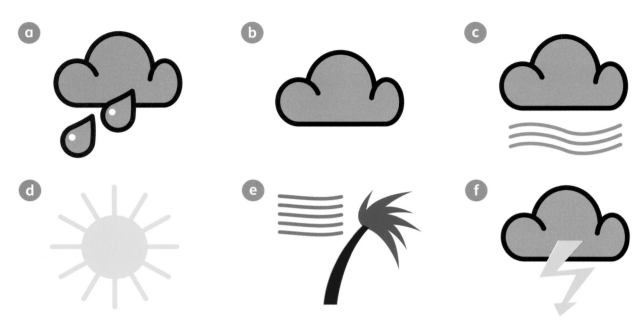

a  b  c

d  e  f

| Monday | Tuesday | Wednesday | Thursday | Friday | Saturday |
|--------|---------|-----------|----------|--------|----------|
| b | ☐ | ☐ | ☐ | ☐ | ☐ |

**2** 🎧 **20** Listen. Are sentences 1–6 true or false?

1 Next week, Bella is going to the beach. `t`

2 Zack's grandparents live in the mountains. ☐

3 It's going to be sunny in the mountains. ☐

4 Zack is going to take Bella's dog for a walk. ☐

5 Bella is going to swim in the sea every day. ☐

6 Zack and Bella are going to read their new books. ☐

**1** Talk about the weather with a friend. Use the words from the box and your ideas.

> rainy    lightning    sunny    thunderstorm    cold    hot    windy

It's going to be rainy.

You need to take a raincoat and an umbrella.

There's going to be lightning.

You need to stay indoors.

**2** Draw a weather forecast for the weekend. Talk about your forecast.

**3** Show the picture of your forecast to a friend. Ask and answer.

Look – it's going to be cloudy and rainy on Wednesday.

Are you going to stay at home?

No, I'm not. I'm going to go to the cinema with friends!

# Audioscripts

## Welcome Unit page 10

**1 Dan** Hey, Anna. Look at these activities at the Explorers Club. Are you good at climbing trees?

**Anna** Yes, I am! I can climb the big tree in my garden with my cousins.

**Dan** Hmm … I'm not very good at climbing trees.

**2 Anna** Look at this one, Dan – horse riding. Are you good at riding horses?

**Dan** No, I'm not. Horse riding is difficult! What about you, Anna?

**Anna** I'm good at it! My uncle and aunt have got horses on their farm.

**3 Dan** Hey, look! We can swim in the sea, too!

**Anna** Oh, I'm very good at swimming in a pool, but I'm not good at swimming in the sea …

**Dan** Really? I'm very good at swimming in the sea. I love it!

**4 and 5**

**Anna** Let's see – oh, kites! Are you good at flying a kite, Dan?

**Dan** No, I'm not, but my sister is really good at it.

**Anna** I'm good at flying a kite, but I'm not very good at riding a bike.

**Dan** Oh, I'm really good at riding my bike, Anna! I can teach you!

### 02

**1 Ben** This is a cool tennis racket, Grace. Is it your sister's?

**Grace** No, it isn't. It's my mother's racket. She loves tennis.

**2 Ben** Grace, can I play your brother's guitar?

**Grace** Oh, that isn't my brother's guitar, Ben.

**Ben** Whose is it?

**Grace** It's my father's.

**3 Grace** Do you like this kite, Ben?

**Ben** Oh, yes, I really like it. Let's fly it!

**Grace** Well, it isn't my kite. It's my sister's. Let's go upstairs and talk to her.

**4 Ben** Grace, who is this in the photo on the fridge?

**Grace** Oh, that's Jill. She's my dad's sister.

**Ben** She looks very friendly.

**Grace** She is! Aunt Jill is fantastic.

**5 Grace** Ben, do you want to play a board game?

**Ben** Which one?

**Grace** That one – it's called Magic Numbers. It's my brother's game.

**Ben** Yes, great!

## Unit 1 page 18

**Grandma** How's your new school, Charlie?

**Charlie** Oh, it's great, Grandma! I'm really enjoying it.

**Grandma** Do you like your teacher?

**Charlie** Yes, I do. Miss French is very nice.

**Grandma** That's good. What's your favourite subject? Is it Maths?

**Charlie** No, it isn't! I'm very good at Maths, but I don't like doing number puzzles. I like Science, Music, History … But my favourite subject is English. I really like reading and writing stories.

**Grandma** I know! You're very good at that. Are there any difficult subjects this year?

**Charlie** Well, Geography. I'm not good at remembering the names of cities.

**Grandma** I can help. I can tell you interesting stories about those cities.

**Charlie** Really? That's great, Grandma!

### 04

**Jack** What do you have to do at your school, Lily?

**Lily** Well, I have to wear a uniform.

**Jack** Me too. And I have to arrive at eight o'clock.

**Lily** At eight o'clock? I don't. School starts at nine o'clock for me.

**Jack** Lucky you! And do you have to do homework every day?

**Lily** Well, not every day. We have homework two or three times a week.

**Jack** That's great. Hey, at my school there are lots of clubs. Do you have to go to clubs after school?

**Lily** No, we don't. We can choose to go to a club or not. Oh! I remember a rule – we have to read one book a week.

**Jack** It's the same at my school. And we have to bring our lunch, too.

**Lily** That's nice! You can choose your lunch! I don't have to bring food. I eat in the school canteen.

## Unit 2 page 26

**1 Tony** Are there any tomatoes for our salad, Lucy?

**Lucy** Look on the table. Are there any tomatoes there?

**Tony** Yes! There are some rolls, too.

**Lucy** Great!

**2 Lucy** Are there any vegetables for the soup, Tony?

**Tony** I can't see any, Lucy.

**Lucy** Look at the bottom of the fridge.

**Tony** Oh, yes! There are some carrots, onions and peas.

**3 Bill** There isn't any apple juice in the fridge.

**Girl** Yes, there is, Bill. Look again.

**Bill** Oh, yes! There is some apple juice next to the lemonade.

**4 Girl** I'm hungry, but there isn't any cheese for my roll.

**Bill** Yes, there is some cheese. It's at the top of the fridge, next to the carrots.

**Girl** Oh, yes! Thanks, Bill.

**5 Boy** I'm thirsty. Can I have some water, May?

**May** Yes, there's some water in the cupboard – next to the apple juice.

**Boy** Thanks!

**May** That's OK!

| 6 | Girl | Are there any rolls in the cupboard, Alex? |
| | Alex | Yes, there are some rolls. Would you like one? |
| | Girl | Yes, please. I'm very hungry! |
| | Alex | Me too! |

 06

| 1 | Dad | Shall we have a pizza for dinner, Vicky? |
| | Vicky | I'm not sure, Dad. How about a chicken salad? There are some nice tomatoes in the fridge. |
| | Dad | That's very healthy! Good idea! |
| 2 | Boy | Daisy, how about onion soup for dinner? |
| | Daisy | I like onion soup, but there aren't any onions in the fridge. |
| | Boy | Oh no! |
| | Daisy | I'd like a pizza. We've got everything for that! |
| | Boy | Great idea! |
| 3 | Girl | Shall we have a chicken sandwich for lunch, John? |
| | John | Yes! Let's see … We've got chicken … Oh, but there isn't any bread. |
| | Girl | Oh, right. How about chicken soup? |
| | John | OK! |
| 4 | Mum | Let's have a cheese and salad sandwich, Jim. Is there any cheese in the fridge? |
| | Jim | Yes, there is, Mum. I'd like a cheese sandwich, but I don't want any salad in it, thanks. |
| | Mum | OK. |

## Unit 3 page 34

07

| Mr Cameron | OK, it's your turn, Ann. Tell us, what do you do in the morning before school? |
| Ann | Well, I get out of bed at half past six – that's very early! After that, I have breakfast with my family. We always have it at quarter to seven. Then I get dressed and brush my teeth at quarter past seven. My brother and I take our dog for a walk before school. We go at quarter to eight. My dog, Lizzie, loves going for walks! When we're back, |

I get my bag from my bedroom and put on my jacket. That's at half past eight. My brother and I usually leave the house at quarter to nine and walk to school. That's my morning, Mr Cameron!

 08

| | Jane | Peter, do you help at home? |
| | Peter | Yes, I do, Jane. Well, I try! Hmm, I sometimes wash up after dinner. |
| | Jane | Really? I never wash up, but I usually dry the dishes. And I like cooking with my dad on Fridays. |
| | Peter | Oh, I like cooking, too. It's my favourite thing! My mum and I always cook pasta on Sundays. |
| | Jane | Mmm … Yummy! Hey, do you help to tidy up the house? |
| | Peter | Well, I tidy up my bedroom … |
| | Jane | Me too, but I also like helping my mum and dad on Sunday mornings. I usually sweep the kitchen and bathroom floors. |
| | Peter | Really? I don't! I don't like tidying up, Jane. I prefer to play with my friends! |

## Unit 4 page 42

 09

| 1 | Girl | Excuse me. Can you help me, please? |
| | Man | Yes, of course. |
| | Girl | Where's the cinema? |
| | Man | Can you see that tower? |
| | Girl | Yes. It's very tall! |
| | Man | Well, the cinema is next to it. |
| | Girl | Thanks! |
| 2 | Boy | Where's the bus station, Mum? |
| | Mum | It's in front of the park. Remember? |
| | Boy | Are we near it? |
| | Mum | Yes! We're only five minutes away. |
| | Boy | Great! My legs are really tired! |
| 3 | Girl | Connor, is the funfair behind the car park or the supermarket? |
| | Connor | The car park. |
| | Girl | Are you sure? I can't see it on my map. |
| | Connor | Look – there it is. |
| | Girl | Oh, yes! |

| 4 | Boy | Excuse me. Do you know the Valley Sports Centre? |
| | Girl | Yes. I go there every weekend. |
| | Boy | Where is it? |
| | Girl | You're very near. Can you see the bank? |
| | Boy | Hmm … yes. It's next to the park. |
| | Girl | Well, the sports centre is behind the bank. |
| | Boy | Thank you! |
| | Girl | You're welcome! |
| 5 | Girl | Excuse me. Can you help me, please? |
| | Woman | Yes, of course. |
| | Girl | Where's the market? |
| | Woman | Oh, I'm sorry, I don't know. Have a look at the map of the town. |
| | Girl | OK. Where's that? |
| | Woman | Opposite the train station. |
| 6 | Boy | Where's the river, Sara? |
| | Sara | I don't know. Perhaps it's near the café. |
| | Boy | Oh, look. There it is! |
| | Sara | Below the castle! Great! |

10

| 1 | Girl | Hey, Oliver. Where are you going? |
| | Oliver | To the clothes shop, with Mum. |
| | Girl | What do you need to get? |
| | Oliver | Black trousers for school. Last year's are small! |
| 2 | Girl | Are you going to the bus station, Dylan? |
| | Dylan | Yes, I am. |
| | Girl | Me too! Where are you going? |
| | Dylan | To my grandpa's house. The bus leaves at five. |
| 3 | Boy | Dad, Where are you going? |
| | Dad | I'm going to the market before it closes! |
| | Boy | Why? |
| | Dad | To get vegetables for our soup! Do you want to come? |
| | Boy | No, thanks. |
| 4 | Boy | Hi, Holly. I'm going to the sports centre. How about you? |
| | Holly | Me too! I'm going to play basketball with my cousin. Look – this is my new ball. |
| | Boy | Wow! It's great! |

**5** **Boy** Hello, Julia. Where are you going?

**Julia** I'm going to the shop to get my dad a book.

**Boy** Is it a present?

**Julia** Yes! It's my dad's birthday tomorrow!

**6** **Girl** Hey, Joe. Are you going home?

**Joe** No, I'm not. I'm going to Liam's house to play his new computer game. Would you like to come?

**Girl** Yes! That sounds great! I love computer games.

## Unit 5 page 50

Hello! My name's Mia. On Saturday afternoon, I was at the Sea Life Centre with my parents. The Sea Life Centre gives a home to some sea animals in danger. It's a really interesting place. There were lots of animals to see! There was a big orange octopus and a beautiful turtle. They were near some starfish. And there was a shark! Mum and Dad were scared of the shark, but I wasn't. It was really small. My favourite sea creatures are seahorses and seals. This time there weren't any, but the dolphins were a nice surprise – they were very friendly! It was a great day and I want to go back to the Sea Life Centre soon!

**1** **Girl** Were you at home yesterday, Leo?

**Leo** No, I wasn't. Do you know the Sea Life Centre?

**Girl** Yes, I do. It's great!

**Leo** Well, I was there with my uncle and aunt.

**2** **Girl** Where were you yesterday, George?

**George** In the sea!

**Girl** In the sea? Wow!

**George** Yes, I was in the sea with my cousins. There were seals all around us. It was fantastic!

**3** **Boy** Were you at the park yesterday, Amy?

**Amy** No, I wasn't.

**Boy** Where were you, then?

**Amy** I was at the cinema. There was a great film on! It was about a shark.

**4** **Boy** Hey, Penny! Were you at the cinema yesterday?

**Penny** No, I wasn't. There weren't any good films on.

**Boy** Where were you?

**Penny** I was at the beach. There were shells everywhere! I like collecting shells.

**5** **Eva** Hi. Guess where I was yesterday.

**Boy** Hmm … Were you at the beach, Eva?

**Eva** No, I wasn't. I was at a party. Look at this photo!

**Boy** Ha! You were a starfish!

**6** **Paul** Yesterday was a great day.

**Girl** Really? I want to hear about it, Paul!

**Paul** Well, I was at home with my brother and sister. *Creatures of the Sea* was on TV!

**Girl** Oh, that's a cool show!

## Unit 6 page 58

**1** **Girl** Wow! Look at this laptop.

**Boy** It's nice, but it's expensive.

**Girl** You're right. What about this one? It's cheaper.

**Boy** I'm not sure … Shall we look in a different shop?

**2** **Ben** Mum, can I have an electric one?

**Mum** Why do you want an electric one?

**Ben** Well, I'm not very good at cleaning my teeth. This one can help.

**Mum** OK, Ben.

**3** **Lucy** Dad, I think the black one is more beautiful than the white one.

**Dad** I agree, Lucy. I think the black one is the best phone. Let's get it.

**4** **Boy** What about this one?

**Girl** Hmm … It's small. We need a bigger one.

**Boy** Well, all of these fans are really small.

**Girl** Oh, look at that fan! It's bigger!

**5** **Carla** This one is nicer.

**Boy** Yes, and it's better than the grey one.

**Carla** It's cheaper, too.

**Boy** Great! It's the tablet for us, Carla!

**6** **Boy** Why do you want this one?

**Girl** Well, this games console is faster than my old one.

**Boy** Hmm … Let's see … How much is it? Oh, look! I think this is the most expensive games console in the shop!

🎧 14

**1** **Suzie** Is your new laptop bigger than mine, Sam?

**Sam** I don't know. Let's take a look.

**Suzie** Ah, mine is bigger!

**Sam** Yes, your laptop is bigger, Suzie!

**2** **Alex** I like the white clock, Fay. Do you?

**Fay** Yes, I do. But look – the blue one is more beautiful, Alex.

**Alex** Hmm … Hey, look at the red one. I think it's more beautiful than the white and the blue clocks.

**Fay** You're right! Let's get that red clock!

**3** **Girl** Is this green mobile phone the best?

**Boy** I don't know. But I know one thing: it's the most expensive!

**Girl** Yes, it is!

**4** **Girl** Here's a torch – look.

**Boy** Thanks, but this black torch is big and heavy. We've got a smaller torch, but I can't find it.

**Girl** What colour is it?

**Boy** Brown.

**Girl** Look, here it is!

**5** **Girl** Excuse me. How much is this orange walkie-talkie?

**Man** It's £25.

**Girl** Hmm … That's expensive.

**Man** I see … How about this yellow one? It's £15.

**6** **John** Let's play with your games console, Gwen. It's better than mine.

**Gwen** Why? I think your games console is fine, John.

**John** Yes, it's OK, but it's slower than yours.

# Unit 7 page 66

 15

| | |
|---|---|
| **Aunt Helen** | Hello, Nick? It's Aunt Helen here. How are you? |
| **Nick** | Oh, hi, Auntie Helen. Well, I'm in bed now. I've got a cold. |
| **Aunt Helen** | Poor you! You've got a bad cold, your mum said. Are you taking any medicine? |
| **Nick** | Yes, Dad gave me some medicine. I've got a headache and a cough, too. Last night I felt terrible! |
| **Aunt Helen** | Oh, I'm sorry, Nick. I hope you feel better soon. Your cousin is ill, too. |
| **Nick** | Oh, what's the matter with Julian, Auntie? |
| **Aunt Helen** | He woke up with a stomach-ache this morning, and he's got earache, too. He's at the doctor's now, with Uncle Chris. |
| **Nick** | Say hello to him. I hope he gets better soon, too. |
| **Aunt Helen** | Thanks, Nick. You and Julian need a rest. Enjoy being at home! Hey, how's your hand? Is it better? |
| **Nick** | Well, my hand was better yesterday … but today it hurts again! |
| **Aunt Helen** | Oh, Nick! |

16

Hi! Last Saturday, lots of things happened, some bad things but some good ones, too. I went to the park with my friends. We played football and I was the goalkeeper. My friend Thomas kicked the ball at me. I jumped for the ball and got it, but I landed on my knee … Ouch! It really hurt! My dad gave me some ice to put on my knee. I felt better, but we went home. I was very angry! But then, my favourite football team was on TV and I watched the match with my mum and dad. It was exciting! And after that, I played computer games with my sister and we had lots of fun. When I went to bed, my knee was OK and I wasn't angry anymore.

# Unit 8 page 74

17

| | | |
|---|---|---|
| **1** | **Boy** | Hi, Vicky! How was your trip? |
| | **Vicky** | It was fantastic! |

| | | |
|---|---|---|
| | **Boy** | What did you visit in Istanbul? |
| | **Vicky** | We didn't go to Turkey. We went to Brazil! |
| **2** | **Girl** | Did you go to Egypt this summer, Karl? |
| | **Karl** | Yes, I did! |
| | **Girl** | Cool! Where did you stay? |
| | **Karl** | Cairo! It's a great place! |
| **3** | **Boy** | Did you have fun in China, Liz? |
| | **Liz** | China? |
| | **Boy** | Yes! You were there in August. |
| | **Liz** | No, I wasn't! I went to Buenos Aires, in Argentina! |
| **4** | **Girl** | Tony, where did I go for Christmas? Guess! |
| | **Tony** | Hmm … I don't know. Spain? |
| | **Girl** | Yes! I went to Madrid. |
| | **Tony** | Really? Me too! I went to see my grandparents. They're from Madrid! |
| **5** | **Boy** | Hi, Meg. How are you? |
| | **Meg** | Really tired! We came back late from our trip last night. |
| | **Boy** | Where did you go? |
| | **Meg** | Istanbul. I loved Turkey! |
| **6** | **Girl** | How was your holiday, Simon? |
| | **Simon** | It was amazing! |
| | **Girl** | Have you got any photos? |
| | **Simon** | Sure. Look – this is Beijing. |
| | **Girl** | Wow! I want to go to China! |

18

| | |
|---|---|
| **Mary** | Did you enjoy your trip to Mexico, Grandpa Joe? |
| **Grandpa** | Ha! I didn't go to Mexico, Mary. I went to India! |
| **Mary** | Oh, yes! I remember now. What did you see there? |
| **Grandpa** | Well, I visited different cities: Jaipur, Mumbai, Bangalore … I travelled by bus and car, and sometimes by plane – India is a big country. One of the biggest in the world! |
| **Mary** | Wow! I want to go! Hey, did you make any friends? |
| **Grandpa** | Of course! I travelled with a group of 15 people. They were all very friendly. They liked my stories about my lovely family! |
| **Mary** | I like your stories, Grandpa! And did you all stay in the same hotels? |
| **Grandpa** | Yes. That was fun! I liked the hotels. They were nice and small. I don't like big hotels. |

| | |
|---|---|
| **Mary** | I know, Grandpa! I'm happy you're back. Your trip was long – one month! |
| **Grandpa** | I'm happy to see you too, dear. Well, I was in India only for two weeks. Remember? Then I went to the countryside. |
| **Mary** | Oh, yes, that's right … Well, one day I want to travel with you, Grandpa. |
| **Grandpa** | Me too, Mary. Where would you like to go? |
| **Mary** | Well, I want to go to Australia to see kangaroos, koalas and … |

# Unit 9 page 82

19

Hello! My name's Finn. I'm very excited because I'm going to Mexico with my family tomorrow. We're going for six days! There's only one problem: the weather! It isn't looking very good … We arrive on Monday. It's not going to be sunny that day – it's going to be cloudy. Then on Tuesday, it's going to be foggy. It's not going to be foggy on Wednesday, but it's going to rain all day! Then on Thursday, it's going to be windy and … there's going to be a thunderstorm on Friday! Now, what's the weather going to be like on Saturday, our last day in Mexico? Well, on Saturday, it's going to be sunny! Arghhh!

20

| | |
|---|---|
| **Zack** | Are you going to the beach next week, Bella? |
| **Bella** | Yes, I am! What about you, Zack? |
| **Zack** | I'm going to stay with my grandparents. They live in the mountains. |
| **Bella** | Wow, that sounds great! |
| **Zack** | Yes, I love it. The beach is fun, too! |
| **Bella** | Yes, I like the sea and the sun. It's going to be sunny all week! |
| **Zack** | Enjoy! It isn't sunny in the mountains – it's usually cloudy, and sometimes it rains. But I don't mind. I love going hiking with my grandparents. And they've got a dog now! I'm going to take their dog for a walk. |
| **Bella** | That's nice, Zack! I'm going to swim in the sea every day and read my new book, *The Thunderstorm*. |
| **Zack** | Guess what? I bought *The Thunderstorm* yesterday and I'm going to read it too! |
| **Bella** | Wow! Haha! |

# Acknowledgements

The authors and publishers acknowledge the following sources of copyright material and are grateful for the permissions granted. While every effort has been made, it has not always been possible to identify the sources of all the material used, or to trace all copyright holders. If any omissions are brought to our notice, we will be happy to include the appropriate acknowledgements on reprinting and in the next update to the digital edition, as applicable.

Key: ST = Starter, U = Unit

**Photography**

The following images are sourced from Getty Images.

**ST**: dobok/iStock/GettyImages Plus; Rob Lewine/Tetra Images; Mark Hall/The Image Bank; Master-Garry/iStock; Francesco Milanese/iStock; ElementalImaging/E+; Jeffrey Coolidge/DigitalVision; Andrea Colarieti/EyeEm; **U1**: Kali9/E+; Tim1743/iStock; FatCamera/iStock; Besjunior/iStock/Getty Images Plus; Mikael Vaisanen/Corbis; Gary John Norman/Cultura; Johner Images; David Buffington/Blend Images; victoshafoto/iStock/GettyImages Plus; IPGGutenbergUKLtd/iStock/GettyImages Plus; Daniel Grill; Westend61; Jennifer Friel Moore/Moment, Peter Dazeley/The Image Bank; **U2**: Westend61; Michael Prince/Corbis; Zing Images/DigitalVision; Kin Images/Photographer's Choice; Joy Skipper/Photolibrary; Westend61; Ezhukov/iStock/Getty Images Plus; Sumit Kumar/EyeEm; Johner Images; **U3**: Peter Dazeley/Photographer's Choice; Stefan Cristian Cioata/Moment; KidStock/Photodisc; DigitalVision; Jose Luis Pelaez Inc/DigitalVision; Ariel Skelley/DigitalVision; MIXA; Simon Watson/The Image Bank; **U4**: RudyBalasko/iStock Editorial/Getty Images Plus; Imgorthand/E+; Nina Erhart/EyeEm/EyeEm Premium; Jose Luis Pelaez Inc/DigitalVision; Comstock Images/Stockbyte; Image Source; mamahoohooba/iStock/Getty Images Plus; Lepro/iStock/Getty Images Plus; Bogdan Vija/EyeEm; Science Photo Library; Glow Images, Inc; johavel/iStock/Getty Images Plus; Issaurinko/iStock/Getty Images Plus; pagadesign/E+; ChristopherBernard/E+; **U5**: Yusuf Kayaoğlu/500px; falcon0125/Moment; A. Martin UW Photography/Moment; Frederic J. Brown/AFP; T. Nakamura Volvox Inc./Oxford Scientific; Jeff Hunter/Photographer's Choice; daniilphotos/iStock/Getty Images Plus; Ed Burns/EyeEm; cristianl/E+; JupiterImages/Polka Dot/GettyImages Plus; **U6**: buz/iStock/Getty Images Plus; gorodenkoff/iStock/Getty Images Plus; luismmolina/E+; kevinjeon00/E+; vectorplusb/iStock/Getty Images Plus; Bigmouse108/iStock/Getty Images Plus; Thomas-Soellner/iStock/Getty Images Plus; SolStock/E+; **U7**: Drazen_/E+; Maskot; dualstock/iStock/Getty Images Plus; MarsBars/iStock/Getty Images Plus; Arnon Mungyodklang/iStock/Getty Images Plus; CiydemImages/E+; filadendron/E+; **U8**: Jean-Pierre Lescourret/Lonely Planet Images; ugurhan/E+; Chad Ehlers/Photographer's Choice; Marwa Morgan/Moment; repistu/iStock/Getty Images Plus; Noppasin Wongchum/iStock/Getty Images Plus; Lane Oatey/Blue Jean Images; Imgorthand/E+; Dougal Waters/DigitalVision; Stephen Lux/Cultura; wrangel/iStock/Getty Images Plus; stock_colors/E+; simonbradfield/iStock Unreleased; Interim Archives/Archive Photos; **U9**: Hispanolistic/E+; sorbetto/DigitalVision Vectors; SW Productions/Stockbyte/Getty Images Plus.

The following images are sourced from other sources/libraries.

**U1**: FogStock/Alamy Stock Photo; **U2**: oznuroz/Shutterstock.

**Illustrations**

A Corazon Abierto (Sylvie Poggio Artists); David Belmonte; Kelsey Collings; Jeff Crowther; Mark Duffin; EMC Design limited; Christina Forshay; Anna Hancock (Beehive Illustration); James Hart (Sylvie Poggio Artists); Marek Jagucki; Graham Kennedy; Andres Martinez Ricci (The Organisation); Alex Patrick; Alan Rowe; David Russell; Debbie Ryder; Savi (Apple Agency), Michelle Simpson; Pipi Sposito; Dave Williams (Bright Agency).

**Audio**

All the audio clips are sourced from Getty Images.

Cedric Hommel/Sound Effects; Trevor Jones/Sound Effects; Sound Effects; Reinhard Wedemeyer/Sound Effects.

Audio produced by Hart McLeod.

**Typeset**

EMC Design limited.